MANTOR

A Layman's Guide to Mentoring at Risk Young Men

By

Andrew McWade

2

For Trenton.....

4

Table of Contents

Table of Contents

Preface

"It is easier to build strong children
than to repair broken men."
-Frederick Douglass

We should always leave things in better condition than we found them. This is especially true when applied to our relationships with children. I believe we have a responsibility to make a positive impact on people's lives if we can, to pass on knowledge and wisdom to those who are willing to receive it, and to help guide those who may have lost their way.

Through education, volunteering, employment, and personal relationships, I have worked with and mentored at risk young men for many years. I have made mistakes that I will hopefully help you to avoid. I have developed some techniques of my own and gleaned wisdom from others that I will pass on to you in this short book. This book is not meant as a technical manual or authoritative text book. This book is a mentoring tutorial, if you will, from someone who has had some success getting through to and mentoring young men. Using some humor and borrowed quotes from wiser men/women than myself, I present this book as a basic tutorial to help you get started on your daunting and rewarding adventure. I commend you for even considering sticking your neck out in order to help someone you do not have to. It takes a village to raise a child, but only one thing can forge a good man, for that, you need a.......MANTOR

> *"If you want to know what a man is like,*
> *take a good look at how he treats his inferiors,*
> *not his equals."*
> *- Serius Black/J.K. Rowling*

The Goal

Congratulations! It's a boy! You didn't make him, but he is yours now. Choosing to become a mentor and make a positive impact on the life of an at risk young man is commendable. By making this decision, you have opened yourself up to potential heartbreak, awkward conversations, infuriating situations, and disappointment. So, why in the world would you or anyone else put themselves out there like that? Because the rewards far outweigh the risks. By making this decision, you have also opened yourself up to feelings of pride, gratification, and accomplishment. You will build friendships with, and leave an ongoing legacy that will be passed down to future generations by the young men you have influenced. You will be immortal! Well, maybe not, but making a difference feels good, and feeling like you were a contributing factor to an at risk young man turning his life around, feels great!

The circumstances in which you have entered your padawan's life may vary. You may have chosen to volunteer for an organization. This could be part of a new career for you, where you will be mentoring a group of guys, or perhaps a personal relationship has thrown you into the orbit of a young person who stares at you suspiciously. Circumstances will of course have some impact on your relationship and interaction, but the same basic principals will apply, or can be tailored to your situation.

Our goal as Mantors is not unlike that of a parent. We are here to teach, counsel, advise, and encourage. We strive to set an example by our own actions, words, and responses to situations and adversities. We want to give these kids the tools they need in order to evaluate a situation and make the correct choice, or at least come to a well thought out conclusion on their own. Our voice should be the voice of reason they hear inside their heads when they are about to do something stupid. We are to be Yoda, Mr. Miyagi, and Master Splinter all in one.

Mantors are not perfect people and do not pretend to be. In fact, the more mistakes you have made, the more times you have been knocked down, the more of life's trials and tribulations you have faced and come out the other side of, the better Mantor you will be. Wisdom is built through experiences, both positive and negative, but more teachable moments arise from defeat than victory. You either win or you learn. The failures and heartbreaks you have endured in your own life will be your most valuable tools when mentoring a young man. For example, one day this kid is going to come to you "snot bubbles crying" because some girl broke up with him. "She was the one" he will scream, chest heaving, trying to catch his breath. Our knee jerk reaction to a fourteen year old who thinks the world has ended because Bella broke up with him is to chuckle and say "that's stupid" or "you'll be fine." Don't do that! His emotions are raw and real. We know because we have already lived through this moment that he is being an over dramatic idiot, but so were we at that age when Jennifer broke up with us. Remember how that felt? Yeah, you remember! Use that memory to muster up some empathy. Talk to the lump of soggy sadness in front of you about how you felt at his age. Level with him. Yes it sucks and it hurts, but someday you will meet Jamie. She is the one.

Your goal as a Mantor is never to replace, undermine, or be at odds with the child's primary caregiver, but rather to be an extension of what already exists. Do not interfere with other good people the kid has in his life, even if you disagree with some of their views. In the end, they outrank you, so we must work within the parameters of whoever or whatever governs the situation. By this I mean family rules, social culture, religious practices & philosophies, and the operating procedures of the organization you are volunteering or working for. You will hold a unique spot in this young man's life, somewhere in the grey area between brother, teacher, coach, and friend. This position of trust will allow you to work in partnership with the child's parents or caregiver. He may open up and share more with you than his parents. He may take to heart advice or guidance you give him, even if it is exactly the same thing his family has been telling him. Kids can be weird that way. It is important for you and the other positive influences in his life to be on the same page and to be in communication with each other. You are a team, working together to keep this boy pointed in the right direction.

"There are three ways to ultimate success;
The first way is to be kind.
The second way is to be kind.
The third way is to be kind."
- Mr. Rogers

At Risk?

"There can be no keener revelation of a societies soul, than the way in which it treats its children."

- Nelson Mandela

Now let's get down to business. What do I mean by "at risk?" The term "at risk youth" gets thrown around a lot, and is loosely defined as kids who have had less than ideal childhoods. As a result, they may be less likely to transition into becoming successful adults. This is an over simplified blanket statement, and you cannot learn anything from over simplified blanket statements. We are going to dive into some of the most common contributing factors, situations, and traumas that lead to a youth being classified as "at risk".

Understanding what type of trauma a kid has been through is perhaps the most important piece of information you will need to know in order to connect with them. The second piece of the puzzle is knowing how to interact with someone who has been through that particular type of trauma. Triggers are real, and if you don't know how to avoid them, things can go south quickly.

Let's look at some of the most common types of childhood trauma, how these kids tend to respond to adults, and some basic do's and dont's to help you avoid pitfalls while attempting to relate to a kid who has been through some stuff. Let's tiptoe through the minefield together.

Physical Abuse: Physical abuse is generally defined as any non-accidental injury of a child. For example; striking, burning, or biting the child. Physically abused kids may have trouble with or even fear developing an attachment to an adult. They may suffer from low self-esteem or have a poor sense of self-worth. Anxiety when around any form of conflict is also common. In their experience, conflict leads to violence, usually towards them. Sadly, the frustrations of parental conflict in violent households is often taken out on the child. These kids may wince or flinch at fast movements. Do not engage in any sort of play fighting with a physically abused child. I am not a big fan of grown men roughhousing or wrestling with young men they are mentoring anyway. We will touch more on that later, but it is especially unacceptable with an abuse survivor. Playful punching in the arm or shoving should absolutely be avoided as well. When a person has been physically dominated in their past, any form of aggression can trigger the emotions they felt as a victim of abuse. This includes yelling and any form of threat, even jokes. For example

"I'm gonna beat you up if you don't finish your ice cream." Some of this may seem silly, but this kid does not know or trust you yet. If you cause them to feel some type of way by trying to be funny or macho, they will slam an emotional door in your face and build a wall in front of it.

Sexual Abuse: Sexual abuse of a child includes, but is not limited to sexual activity with a minor (rape). This also includes sex trafficking, inappropriate photography, an adult exposing themselves to a child, or sharing pornographic material with a minor. All of these examples of sexual abuse and molestation can do irreparable damage to a young person, leaving deep, life-long scars. Young men who have been sexually abused may feel a sense of shame or blame themselves for not being "strong enough" to stop it. They may be questioning their own masculinity or even their sexual orientation. Almost anything can be an emotional trigger for survivors of sexual abuse. Something as simple as a smell, location, or a person who happens to resemble their abuser can create extreme emotional reactions within the person. Of course we cannot foresee or control stimuli such as a random smell, but we can be cognizant of our own behaviors and actions that could possibly be triggers. I would advise against any form of physical touch if you are aware a kid has been sexually abused. Something as simple as a pat on the shoulder or even sitting a little too close could send cold chills through the person. You may want to consider outright asking him what he is comfortable with. Something like, "Hey, if you do something awesome and I want to convey that to you, would you prefer a pat on the back, a fist bump, or a thumbs up from across the room?" Also be aware of compliments concerning physical appearance. This person has been victimized and objectified in the worst possible way and are constantly on high alert. Innocent compliments like, "You clean-up nice," or "That shirt looks good on you," could trigger the kid's internal alarms.

Emotional Abuse: Emotional abuse, also known as psychological or verbal abuse, is the most common form of child abuse. Emotional abuse occurs when a child is repeatedly made to feel unloved, worthless, alone or scared. The impacts of emotional abuse are just as harmful as those of physical abuse. Verbally abused kids can have trouble controlling their emotions and anger, may lack self-confidence and can have trouble making and maintaining relationships. Building a relationship with victims of psychological abuse can be especially difficult, because a lot of kids who have suffered through this trauma withdraw emotionally as a defense mechanism. Patience is truly a virtue in this situation. It may take time and lots of positive encouragement to break down the walls and gain the young person's trust. A good way to begin mentoring an emotionally abused kid, is to have them teach you about something they are interested in. This can help build-up their self-worth and confidence. Most kids will begin to come out of their shell if you get them talking about something they are passionate about.

Physical Neglect: Neglect is defined as the failure, refusal, or inability of a parent or caregiver to provide the basic necessities a child needs to survive and thrive. These include basic physical needs like food, shelter, clothing, and medical attention. This category also extends to education and providing a safe living environment with adequate adult supervision. Children of neglect may have low self-esteem from being made fun of at school due to lack of hygiene or appropriate clothing. If the kid suffers with food insecurity, he may hoard food. For example, I once mentored a young man, and whenever I took him to a diner or restaurant, he would fill his pockets with saltines, jelly, and anything else he could get his hands on that was technically free. This kid never knew if he would have food at home to eat, so stocking up on things like this was a survival strategy. I always pretended not to notice, as not to embarrass him, but it broke my heart. When dealing with a victim of neglect, I would caution against saying anything negative about the kids parents for two reasons. Number one, it may not have been malicious or even completely the parent or guardians fault. The entire family could be the victims of a financial hardship that is out of their control. Number two, kids are protective of their parents, even if they suck. You will immediately turn a kid against you if you badmouth his folks. I would also advise against buying the kid expensive clothing or shoes. It is ok to want to help out with basic needs, but keep it modest.

Witnessing Parental Abuse: Witnessing violence in the home can be particularly damaging to a kid. Internally it can cause stress and anxiety, leading to stomach problems, headaches, and poor performance at school. It can skew their version of relationships, and what is acceptable behavior. Witnesses of violence are more likely to see violent behavior as the most efficient path to conflict resolution, and are thus more likely to use violence towards others. They may feel guilty for not being able to stop one parent from abusing the other, or feel conflicted regarding which parent they should support. Witnesses of parental abuse tend to respond similarly to victims of physical abuse, so my advice is similar. I would refrain from any form of play fighting or jokes about violence. I would recommend talking with them about what a healthy relationship looks like, and how to handle conflict without violence or screaming like a maniac. As a Mantor, it is one of our responsibilities to teach young men how mature men of character handle conflict. Breaking a cycle of abuse through education and example is definitely something we aim to do.

Household Substance Abuse: Parental substance abuse can have lots of side effects and open the door to other forms of neglect and abuse. Addiction can cause someone to do things they may never do sober, like physically abuse or neglect their child. It can turn a parents attention away from what truly matters, causing financial issues leading to physical neglect. I am of the belief that addiction is a disease and that people should be offered help and a shot at redemption before condemnation. When mentoring a kid who comes from a home with a substance abuser, I recommend focusing most of your attention and efforts on the child. That said, extending a hand in order to help the adult who is struggling with addiction should always be an option in your mind. If you do decide to speak with them, this will be an awkward conversation, which could end badly. Remember, a Mantor's primary concern is helping the young person who is at risk. The best shot at accomplishing that may be to help his family heal. If that is not an option, then continue to be the kid's mentor. Be the healthy dependable adult they need in their life. Be on the lookout for signs of abuse or neglect, and be willing to report them to the authorities.

Household Mental Illness: Having a family member struggling with mental health issues within a household does not necessarily equal danger or trauma for the child. This is a huge topic, that would require its own book in order to properly cover all of the scenarios. The kid may have a parent or sibling who suffers some form of diagnosed mental illness. Depending on severity and treatment, this may have little effect on the child. However; if certain types of mental illness are left untreated, it can be devastating to a family. Be aware of the exact situation and do some research so that you know what the kid is dealing with and what signs you should be looking out for. NAMI.org is an excellent source of information. Regardless of the diagnosis or severity, kids who live in a household where mental illness is present usually have anxiety about being diagnosed themselves. Speak with them about it. Being educated about mental health management can help dispel fear and stigma.

Parent Separation or Divorce: Structure, consistency, stability, and knowing where home is are all extremely important for a child's successful development. A messy divorce can throw all of these necessities into chaos, especially during the transitional period while the parents negotiate what the new normal will look like. Kids can be an unfortunate casualty in divorce proceedings and are often used as leverage or outright weaponized by the parents. This can lead to the child blaming themselves for the divorce, even though they may have nothing at all to do with the decision. They may be pulled in two directions, feeling as though they have to pick one parent over the other. When mentoring a child who's parents are having trouble, it is obviously important to impress upon them that it is not their fault, and that both parents love him. Be ready for him to cry and rant about the situation. People need to vent, but the thing people need the most when their world is in chaos is a point of reference. Something that is stable and consistent. Be the calm in the storm the kid needs in that moment.

Incarcerated Family Member: Young men tend to idolize their fathers, even if old dad is a criminal. If you are lucky, the father of the young man you are mentoring knows he messed up and encourages his son not to follow in his footsteps. Unfortunately that is not always the case. When you are surrounded by criminal culture as a child, becoming a criminal yourself seems just as natural as joining the family business and is sometimes encouraged. This situation can be an uphill battle for a mentor. You are attempting to change a kid's value system. This is truly a time to be a role-model. You must, over time, show him he can become a different type of man than his incarcerated family member. Present alternative choices and viewpoints from what he is accustomed to.

Never talk bad about the incarcerated person. Nothing good can come from that. Just be the man you are, and hopefully the kid will begin to emulate your example and turn away from criminality.

Growing up is hard under ideal circumstances. Dealing with any of the above risk factors with a still forming brain, overactive hormones, and just overall teenage awkwardness is a tall order for anyone to overcome. These guys can use all the help they can get while attempting to navigate through the rough uncertain waters of adolescence. Help them unpack and process some of the baggage they are carrying. Teach them alternative solutions and philosophies. Help them to develop coping skills and problem solving abilities, and remember that "at risk" does not mean doomed to fail.

"You, me, or nobody is gonna hit as hard as life.
But it ain't about how hard ya hit.
It's about how hard you can get hit and keep moving forward.
That's How Winning Is Done!"
- Rocky Balboa

Shut Up & Listen

"We have two ears and one mouth,
so we can listen twice as much as we speak."
-Epictetus

How would you feel if a total stranger stomped up to you, announced they were your new mentor and then started telling you how to live your life? It would be pretty weird and off putting wouldn't it? So, maybe don't do that. It is great to be excited and fired up about becoming a mentor….sorry….Mantor, but fight off the urge to jump right in there and start doling out sage like advice right off the bat. It will freak the kid out, I promise.

If you want to make a difference in someone's life, you have got to get to know them first. The best way to do that is to ask them questions, and then, you guessed it, shut up and listen. This might sound easy, but there are strategies to not only asking questions, but also listening properly to the answers. Kids have a tendency to answer questions using as few words as possible, especially when they do not know the inquisitor very well. Because of this, you will want to ask open ended questions. This will make it more difficult for them to provide you with one word answers. If you let them, a kid will have an entire conversation with the words yes, no, and fine. So, instead of asking, "Did you have a good day at school?" Leaving yourself open for a classic "It was fine." Try something like, "Tell me about the best thing that happened at school today." This will encourage him to give you a multiple word explanation. When he does begin to communicate with you using full sentences, it is important for you to be an active listener. When people open up, they want to feel heard. Be an engaged audience. Make the kid feel like you care about what he has to say. A good way to do this is to occasionally repeat or "parrot" part of a sentence back to them. Nod your head and smile like a human. Ask follow-up questions, and be interested in learning about the young man's life. Open posture and body language are also important, so uncross your arms and relax. Over seventy percent of communication is nonverbal. Be aware of that and the message you are sending with your posture, arm placement, and eye contact. Once you have broken the communication ice and developed an open honest dialogue with the kid, you can begin teaching, coaching, and mentoring him.

I stated earlier that one of our goals is to give these young men the tools they need in order to evaluate, think through their options, and make what they feel the correct choice is on their own. The word correct can be subjective of course. Your desired outcome may be different than mine, but both can be positive. We are encouraging them to avoid negative outcomes whenever possible. The best way to teach this skill is to regularly engage in critical thinking exercises with your padawan. You could start small with something like evaluating what to have for lunch before you go on a run. Present him with three choices like a healthy salad & water, pizza & soda, or all the ice cream we can eat. He can pick one of the three choices for lunch, but you are both one hundred percent going on a run afterwards. Look at factors such as the nutritional value, enjoyment level, cost and the potential side effects or consequences these meals may have on your run. Shut up and listen. Let him think it through aloud, and let him decide. After his research is complete and the choices have been weighed, turn him loose to make the decision and to experience the effects of his choice. Whether you two have a successful run due to him correctly evaluating and wisely choosing salad, or you both end up with the bubble guts, something will be learned and a conversation will be had. These exercises will help teach him lessons like instant gratification vs long term thinking and the importance of including logic when making decisions, instead of just going with what you feel or what you want. Sacrificing the instant gratification you want (ice cream) for the logical choice with long term benefits (salad) could keep you from embarrassingly blowing chunks on the jogging path. Encourage and help him utilize this same technique to evaluate all of the decisions and situations in his life. You guys can talk through every decision from what club or sport to join, who to ask on a date, what type of car he should get or what college and major to choose.

Another good habit to instill is self evaluation. Sit down with your mentee after he has competed or participated in something, or after an event like a date. Ask him to provide you with three things he did well, and three things he could have done better. For example, let's say the kid is on the basketball team and had a game yesterday, so you sit him down and ask him our patented two sided question. He responds with, I led the team in rebounds, played lock down defense, and scored twenty points. However, I missed all my free throws, fouled out in the third quarter and hit a cheerleader in the face with a bad pass. This self evaluation identified opportunities for self improvement. You guys can now hit the gym to practice free throws, passing and talk about how to avoid mental mistakes like fouls. You should also pick up an apology card on the way to the gym for him to give to the cheerleader he maimed.

When I make the statement "Shut up and Listen," it is not just about us as adults taking the time to listen to a kid in order to get to know him. The bigger picture is us encouraging him to verbalize his thoughts and develop communication skills. We are teaching skills that will benefit this young man throughout his life. Having the ability to verbally evaluate a situation with others is extremely valuable in the workplace. We are also developing his ability to look inward and to evaluate his own behavior and performance. Just being willing and able to do this will grow his emotional maturity, but putting that information to work in order to improve himself is what will make him an all around better person.

Public speaking is one of the most common fears people share. I would go as far as to say most people have anxiety about standing in front of a group of people to give a speech or presentation, so anyone who overcomes this fear will have an advantage, especially in the workplace. When we encourage him to speak while we shut up and listen, we are developing his oratory skills as well as building his confidence. Being well spoken and articulate will open doors for him, and just like any other skill, requires practice and repetition. Our long term goal is for him to be comfortable addressing a crowd of people. Look for or create opportunities for him to speak in front of small groups of people at first. For example, if he has an oral report or presentation he is working on for school, have him give his presentation to you and a hand full of other people he knows. Practicing in front of people he is already comfortable around and who care about him will help build his confidence. Once he is comfortable with that core group, invite some people he does not know to join the audience, and you can all shut up and listen together. As his skills and confidence grows encourage him to pursue leadership roles at school or church.

While I was an advisor for a youth organization, one of my favorite exercises to help develop these skills was to hold mock job interviews. We would have the boys pick an occupation, fill out a generic application, and then we would interview them using behavioral based interview questions. These are multi part questions that really force the person to lay out a story from beginning to end. For example "Bob, tell us about a time you had a disagreement with a coworker. What was the disagreement? How did you handle the situation? What was the final resolution?" We would ask the boys several of these questions with all the seriousness of a potential employer, even if the kid chose a ridiculous career. I have stone faced asked a thirteen year old "It says here you are applying to be King of the Universe, what attributes and experiences to you posses that would make you the best fit for this positions over the other applicants?" I have received some surprisingly good and astonishingly stupid answers over the years, but that is irrelevant. The goal is to develop his speaking skills.

> *"It is very important in life to know when to shut up.*
> *You should not be afraid of silence."*
> *-Alex Trebek*

Darkness Avoid

"You underestimate the power
of the Dark Side."
- Darth Vader

Bonding with the young men we mentor is natural and encouraged. It is human nature to begin seeing them as more of a friend and less of a student. In fact we want these guys as life long friends. However; we must remember that they are kids, and not our buddies. Do not confide in or have inappropriate conversations with them. We are not to burden them with our troubles or forget where the line is when it comes to certain subjects. Let's go over a few topics to avoid. Topics that may bring out your......dark side.

Drugs & Alcohol: We are adults, and probably have a drink or two every now and then. It is also possible we have struggled with addiction in our lives. Back in the day we may have even done some dangerous, stupid, entertaining or downright hilarious stuff while under the influence of whatever. None of that is any of this kid's business, and it is ok to tell him just that. You don't need to lie, or pretend to be a perfect person, but you also don't need to share everything with him. Telling him about your wilder days will just glorify and justify drug and alcohol use to him. Keep in mind that he probably looks up to you by now, and may try to emulate your behavior, even past bad behavior. It is perfectly fine to put a pin in certain conversations until your young friend graduates college. Until then, toe the line. No booze until you are twenty-one, even then drink responsibly, and drugs are bad… mkay.

Criminal Activity: This guy may be from a rough neighborhood, maybe its the same one you are from. When you grow up around criminals and criminal activity it becomes normalized, accepted, expected, and sometimes even encouraged. Pulling someone out of this culture is very difficult, and changing their values system is even harder. Messaging must remain consistent on this subject to have any chance at changing the way he views the world and what type of behavior is acceptable in it. Crime is never funny, and we should never allow or encourage him to tell war stories of his past criminal behavior or gang activity. We have a lot of goals while mentoring someone, but goal number one is keeping them out of the house of many doors.

Sex: Sex takes up more of a teenage boys brain than anything else. Sex is everywhere. It's in the music they listen to, the video games they play, movies, tv, and it is their main topic of conversation with friends. There is literally nothing they think about or want to talk about more. Because of this, they don't need to talk about it with you. Unless you have been asked to give "The Talk" to the boy by his parent or guardian, nothing good can come from talking about sex with him. I encourage you to talk about healthy relationship practices, how to treat someone they are dating, and respecting boundaries, but a grown man talking to a child about having sex with another child is inappropriate and beyond creepy. Also, be careful you don't accidentally get pulled into inappropriate conversations. Locker room talk is a slippery slope.

Religion: Your mentee and his family may not have the same beliefs as you, and that is ok. It is not ok for us to undermine or criticize their belief system, or push any religious views upon them. Mentoring someone with the purpose of evangelizing them is underhanded. We can be a positive influence in this young man's life without having religious debates. Because of this, I tend to avoid religious conversations and sharing my personal beliefs with young men I mentor. Now, if you happen to share the same beliefs system as the young man and his family, then feel free to use your shared faith as a tool for teaching and bonding.

Your Problems: When you have bonded with a young man, it can be hard to not see him as a friend, and friends talk about their problems with each other, right? Wrong! Venting should only go one way, him venting to you. We are there to support and advise him. Burdening him with our problems is not ok. He shouldn't have to worry about our job, marriage or financial situation. What good can come from dumping all of our emotional garbage on this kid? Are you going to take financial or relationship advise from a thirteen year old? He has enough to worry about. Growing up is hard enough without having our crap rattling around in his head too. The only time we should speak to him about a problem we had or are having, is if it can be used to teach him something.

Gossip: You may live in the same town as the young man you are mentoring. Because of this, you need to be careful what you say to him, especially about other people. You may know that his buddy's dad is an alcoholic or that his girlfriend's mom sleeps around. He doesn't need to know what you know. You are also partially responsible for developing his behavioral patterns, so don't teach him that gossip is ok, and nip it in the bud if he starts spreading rumors about people. We should encourage them to reach out and help people who may be struggling with something, not talk about them behind their backs, and if we can't help someone, at the very least, don't hurt them. Gossiping about people hurts them and is cowardly.

Fighting & Violence: Many of us have been in a slobberknocker or two, maybe more. You might even be a trained fighter or soldier. Do you think that is cool? I do, and the kid for sure will. However, this young man may come from a violent environment and may be quick to violence himself. We are tasked with showing him a different way of handling things, so glorifying fighting will only confuse him. Teach him how to use his words. Teach him that walking away is an option and that violence should always be the last resort. Above all, teach him humility through your own actions. Real tough guys don't brag. They don't have to.

"We've all got both light and dark inside of us.
What matters is the part we choose to act on."
- Sirius Black/J.K. Rowling

Keeping Your Word

"Men with good intentions make promises.
Men with good character keep them."
- Ronald Oliver

People as a whole are reluctant to trust one another. Kids are even more reluctant to trust a new adult in their lives, and if that kid has been abused or mistreated, they are usually exceedingly suspicious and standoffish. They expect to be lied to and for promises to be broken. That is why it is so important to keep your word and to honor your promises. If you don't, that kid will relegate you to the pile with every other adult who has hurt or lied to them. Remember our goal as a Mantor is to help him to become a good man, and the best way to do that is to show him what one looks like. Lead by example.

Things that seem insignificant to us, may be a big deal to them. Even breaking small promises can have a huge damaging impact on your relationship, especially in the beginning. If the child learns from the git go, you do not keep your word every single time, they will not trust you. Trust is hard to build, but easily lost. I have also learned from experience that "I forgot" is the worst excuse you can give. Telling a child that you simply forgot about them is damaging. If you do encounter a situation where you honestly forgot about something, use it as a teachable moment. Hold yourself accountable, apologize, and make sure he knows that "I forgot" is a BS excuse. Talk about tools that are available to help us avoid this mistake again.

While working for a residential detention center, I would regularly have kids ask me to take them for walks around the grounds. This was their way of getting away from the chaos of the other boys, in order to vent one on one with a staff member they trusted.

I recall one of my most regular walk requesters was a young man named Mack. He was a camouflage and work boot wearing country boy from a farm town, and would constantly get frustrated with the other boys in the facility who were more "city" than him. He was a tough kid, but very soft hearted and emotional. The type of guy that cries when he is about to fight someone. The detention center was located way out in the country, and the only neighbor had a bunch of cows. This reminded Mack of home, so when he got upset and was ready to stomp a mud hole in some poor city kid and walk it dry. I would take him for walks over by the cow pasture where we would literally moo at the cows just as loud as we could. It must have been quite a sight for anyone passing by to see two guys standing out in the yard screaming Moo! Mack loved it when the cows mooed back. We would do this regularly. We always ended up laughing and then Mack would tell me what was really bothering him and why he freaked out on whoever. These walks were very important to him and I will never forget Mack the cow whisperer.

Going on individual walks helped the boys calm down, process thoughts, and disconnect from the group for a bit. I learned not to "promise" to take someone for a walk unless I was one hundred percent sure it would happen. Kids don't care that you had to break up a fight, chase a runaway or do a bunch of paperwork. All they know is that you promised them something. Going for a walk wasn't a big deal to me, but it was a huge deal to them, especially when they really needed to talk. I could give a hundred examples or cliches about a man's word being his bond or if you shake on something, it is as good as a contract, but this chapter doesn't need to be very long. The bottom line is that what you say matters. Promises matter, and breaking your word to a child hurts them, so just don't do it.

> *"Do, or do not.*
> *There is no try."*
> *- Yoda*

Refocusing Anger & Aggression

"When one has been angry for a very long time, one gets used to it.
And it becomes comfortable, like…like old leather.
And finally…becomes so familiar that one can't
even remember feeling any other way."
- Jean Luc Picard

More often than not, kids who fall into the "at risk" category have endured some sort of trauma, tragedy or mistreatment in their lives, and more often than not, they are pissed off about it. Our job is to identify what type of anger the child is dealing with, and if it is unhealthy anger, try to refocus or divert that energy into something that is more mentally and physically beneficial.

Anger can manifest itself in several ways, and anger is not always a bad thing. Justifiable or righteous anger is normal and healthy. Sometimes being mad as hell about a situation is the correct reaction. For example, anger is a healthy part of the grieving process. Anger is also appropriate if you have been victimized by someone or are a victim of circumstance.

I was mentoring a young man called James. James was the classic tough exterior having smack talker with a soft heart. He had gotten into some trouble and was working his way through a program in order to atone for his transgressions. James had a hair trigger with his anger, and was usually angry for no good reason, or over something that didn't really matter. We had many conversations while he was "mad" that usually ended in laughter, but one time was different. James' father is in prison, potentially for the rest of his life, and James had not seen him for two years. The state had granted and set it up for James to be escorted from our facility to his father's prison for a visit. James was over the moon with excitement. It was all he talked about for weeks leading up to the visit. James trusted me and would read me letters sent between him and his father. I will say, that for all of his faults and bad grammar, James' father loved him and did not want his son to end up in a cage like he did. Two days before the visit was to occur, it was canceled due to a worldwide pandemic. James was devastated. His heart was broken and he was pissed. I had never seen him like this. He was always "mad" and yelling about something, but this time he was silent. I knew that James needed to cry, but would not allow himself to be vulnerable in front of the other boys, so I took him for a walk to help him process his anger. While on our walk he informed me that he already knew what I was going to say, and he didn't want to hear about how "he is being dramatic" or that "Anger clouds judgement." I told him I was actually going to say the opposite. I told him that this whole situation F"ing sucks, and how he has every right to be angry, and that I was mad too. As soon as I said those words he began to cry, it was like he needed permission to let out his true emotions. We had a great conversation that night, and James began working through his initial anger over this crappy situation. That night I taught James the term justifiable anger, and from then on, whenever he got mad, he would ask me if what he was feeling was "justifiable anger?" 99% of the time, it was not. The problem occurs when someone holds on to that anger for too long, and allows it to fester and change them. Eventually they need to be an Elsa, and let it go. If they don't, anger can become a person's defining characteristic.

Talking about and processing the situation with a trusted adult or counselor can help a kid move past the first stages of anger, so that they don't get stuck there. If the boy is willing to talk to you about his anger, then please let him vent and help him make sense of it. Young men tend to struggle with communication and feelings, so if you are seen as a trusted confidant, and you are comfortable talking about the situation with him, you have an opportunity to do a lot of good. Keep in mind, not all situations have a solution. Sometimes life is garbage, but I would rather sit in a dumpster with a friend, than alone.

Aggressive anger is the most common type of anger for young men. In most cases, aggression is just a thin veil guys put up in order to mask insecurity or as a defense mechanism. This type of anger is mostly pretend anger, and is easily identified by the typical chest puffing, constant threats of violence against others, and attempts to look hard and tough to the outside world. Our job is to help Mr. Mean Mug to mature through this stage of his existence. The more self confidence we can help him build, the less he will act like this. People who are comfortable in their own skin don't stomp around wearing the grumpy face. If this is a defense mechanism they have built up because of past mistreatment, the only thing that will break that wall down is time and the realization that everyone is not out to get them, and they should probably just relax. The more good people the young man is exposed to and communicates with, the faster this process will go. I have been blessed with some friends and acquaintances in my life who are legit badasses, soldiers, federal agents, detectives, a UFC hall of famer, and other impressive men. I love bringing young men I mentor around these individuals, because none of these men act or talk tough, they just are. Seeing this, sometimes helps them realize how ridiculous all of their posturing is.

The final type of anger we will cover is no joke. It is that deep, destructive, scary rage some people carry around with them all the time. The type of inner hatred and resentment for humanity that gives others the chills. Young men like this are rare, but they tend to act on their violent and destructive impulses, sometimes without warning. Hopefully this kid is in therapy getting the professional help that is needed. If you are mentoring a young man who fits this description, you have a daunting task ahead of you. I recommend attempting to redirect as much of his rage into something positive as you can. Encourage him to journal about his anger and help him develop coping skills. Attempt getting him into a sport or working out. Things like running or lifting weights can be incredibly beneficial. Getting physically fit can help build self confidence. Also, setting and achieving incremental workout goals will help to draw their attention away from their anger and towards something positive. When looking into potential sports, keep in mind, young men who are struggling with severe anger and aggression usually are not a great fit for team sports like basketball or football, however, they may excel in a more individual sport like wrestling or track.

Hopefully some combination of communication, counseling, athletics, and encouragement can change this young man's outlook on the world before he becomes dangerous.

> *"Holding on to anger is like drinking poison*
> *and expecting the other person to die."*
> *-Paraphrased Buddha Quote*

Building Self Confidence

"I have come here to chew bubble gum and kick ass.
And I'm all out of bubble gum."
- Rowdy Roddy Piper

Few people are born with unwavering self confidence. If you are one of those blessed people who has never ever doubted yourself or any decision you have ever made, Congratulations you are a narcissist! Most people have quietly struggled with self esteem, self image, and self worth issues several times throughout their lives. Unfortunately, a perfect storm of awfulness is created between the ages of thirteen and seventeen. Our bodies, minds, and hormones are all weird and out of control. We are clumsy, emotional, irrational, and awkward. The bright side is that everyone around us is going through the same thing, so we are all super supportive of one another. Am I right? No! Kids are terrible to each other! They are so self conscious about their own situation, they will do and say anything to draw negative attention away from themselves and put it on someone else. Any perceived insecurity or imperfection that presents itself on friend or foe is a potential target for ridicule. Because of this, they are constantly on guard, and constantly judging and evaluating each other. Well, at least they can relax and let their defenses down at home and away from school. No again! They carry their bullies around in their pockets in the form of cell phones. Being a teenager can be a brutal inescapable hell. Some of them silently suffer an endless onslaught of negativity from their peers, and this is just average "normal" kids. At risk kids have all of this plus whatever else is going on in their lives. They may live in an unsafe or difficult environment. They may not have an adequate support system of people helping them through the nightmare that is being a teenager. Any number of situations can contribute to making the already difficult business of growing up, even harder. So, what can we do to help? For starters, we can be a constant source of encouragement. Celebrate every victory and accomplishment with them, even the small ones. Look for, and create situations that will build their self confidence. One of my go to moves, is to discover something the kid is talented at or interested in, and have them teach me about it.

Some time ago, while working in a residential detention center, I mentored a young man named Aiden, who had trouble verbalizing and communicating his feelings. Aiden also had a very fragile ego and self esteem. I wanted to break through to the kid, so I asked him to "teach" me how to play chess. He was thrilled at the prospect of teaching an adult something, so about three times a week, we would sit down, have a chess lesson and talk about life.

The lessons later turned into competitive matches. The tougher I played him, the more the victories meant to the young man, building his self confidence. I also found, that the harder Aiden had to concentrate on the game, the more freely words would come to him and the conversation would flow. We would talk trash to one another before and during the game, then shake hands over the board to thank each other for the match afterwards. In retrospect, pretending not to know how to play chess in order to help this kid develop skills and build confidence was dishonest on my part. If he would have found out the truth, it may have damaged our relationship. I should have found another way to go about it, or had him teach me something I didn't know already. Mantors make mistakes too.

While working in the same detention center, I developed a great relationship with a seventeen year old young man called Travis. Back home he was referred to as Big T. He was self conscious about his weight, but did not know what to do about it. One day I had a one on one conversation with Travis. I told him that since he was stuck in here for the next seven to ten months, he might as well exit/graduate the program sexier than when he entered. We made an agreement. I would teach him how to diet properly, by teaching him about nutrition. I would also set up workout routines for him and lift weights with him at least three hours per week. Travis in turn, would keep his anger under control, and lead the other boys by example. Travis already had natural charisma and leadership abilities. He kept his word and quickly became the undisputed leader of the residents. Travis also dedicated himself to healthy eating and exercise. Our two man weight lifting club began to grow as the residents witnessed Big T's physical transformation. Before long, almost all of the residents were working out with us. Several of the boys made noticeable changes in their physical appearance. These physical changes lead to a rise in body image, self esteem, self confidence, and overall attitude. There is a direct correlation between physical health and mental health. They go hand in hand with each other, so if you can motivate the young man you are mentoring to work out, or get involved in some athletic activity, it will have a positive impact on their mental wellness and self confidence.

Why is self confidence so important? What is the benefit? Confident people tend to have higher standards for how they allow others to treat them. Self assured people are also more able to receive constructive criticism without becoming defensive, evaluate that information, and use it to make changes and improvements. They are comfortable enough to look inward in order to identify faults and weaknesses they need to work on without becoming depressed or breaking down. Confident people attract other confident people into their friend group and are comfortable enough to handle a strong, independent romantic partner who challenges them. Confidence helps a person interview well for internships and employment. Confident people tend to climb social, professional, and political ladders more efficiently, and often become leaders in their communities. That is why confidence is so important, so please do everything in your power to encourage and build up young peoples self confidence every chance you get, because, It's hard out there for a kid.

"Confidence is silent.
Insecurities are loud."
-Unknown

Life Lessons

"It is possible to commit no errors and still lose.
That is not weakness....That is life"
-*Jean Luc Picard*

Some lessons are so important, you should forever keep them in the forefront of your mind. Always be on the lookout for opportunities to reenforce them in your padawan. These things aren't just lessons, they are life lessons. These ideals can have a profound impact on your mentee's life and mindset, if you can get him to take them to heart. Let's go over some of them.

Money does not buy happiness: Comedian Daniel Tosh once said "Money doesn't buy happiness. Uh, do you live in America? Cause it buys a WaveRunner. Have you ever seen a sad person on a wave runner. Have you?" I think most of us would like to take a swing at being fabulously wealthy just to see if it would make us happier. Money can buy a lot of cool stuff and experiences, and it is a tall order to convince a teenage boy that money cannot buy happiness, especially if he grew up in poverty. As mature men, we know things like love, inner peace, fulfillment, and respect cannot be bought. Money cannot buy things that must be earned, and these are the things human beings long for and crave. I am not saying wealth is bad, but sometimes, in the words of the great American poet Notorious B.I.G. "Mo Money Mo Problems."

Eat the elephant one bite at a time: Everyone gets overwhelmed from time to time, but not everyone has developed the tools to deal with the feeling of having an impossible mountain of work in front of them. Some people get filled with anxiety, panic and quit, or worse yet, they don't even try. Whenever a young man I am mentoring is faced with such a situation, whether it is school, work, or relationship related. I always ask them the same question. "How do you eat an elephant?" I ask it so much, that I usually get an eye roll and an exasperated response of "One bite at a time." Thats right, so start chewing! Long term goals are met by breaking a seemingly insurmountable target into small bite sized tasks, and just as pennies make dollars, those bite sized tasks add up to success. This lesson will be easier and easier to reenforce once your mentee has attained success and achieved goals using this philosophy.

You can't please everyone: Almost all people want to be liked, respected, and accepted by others. In a perfect world, we would be more tolerant of one another, and celebrate our differences instead of judging one another so harshly. It can be a hard pill for a kid to swallow when they begin encountering people, especially adults who prematurely judge them or have outright decided they do not like them, especially when the reason for this hatred is something as ignorant as skin color, sexual orientation, how they dress, or just the fact that they are young. High school can be a savage land full of sarcasm, cliques, and labels. This can be a difficult time, but kids tend to have a support group of friends they can retreat to, and are generally accustomed to some of their peers being horrible monsters. Let's move past school, and into the workplace. This is usually a young persons first forced interaction with a random group of people from all age groups with varying cultural, social, religious and political views. Inevitably, your mentee will come to you and say something like, "Karen hates me and I don't know why. I am always nice to her, but no matter what, she treats me like trash." Your first reaction as someone who knows this kids heart and cares about him will be to blurt out, "Well F#%@ Karen!" And in a lot of ways you would be right, but it is not the correct way to handle the situation. Karen wants our guy to fire back with negativity. Karen wants him to be what she has already decided he is. Karen wants him to prove her right, because Karen is the worst person who has ever lived. This is a time where we need to enforce to him that no matter how kind you are to some people and no matter how terrific of a person you are, you can't please everyone. Karens gonna Karen. Do not allow someone to turn you into something you are not. Stay true to yourself and be kind to everyone, especially Karen, because nothing will infuriate her more. God I hate Karen.

Value your health: Teenage boys are invincible, just ask them, and if you talk to an old man they will tell you that youth is wasted on the young. This is because most young people take for granted what us older people know is truly valuable, your health. You only get one body and watching a kid poison his with junk food, soda, and potentially drugs all while not exercising is infuriating to someone who's knees pop when they get up to take their thyroid medicine. Most of us wish we would have taken better care of our bodies in our youth, but that time has passed. We can, however, attempt to impart the importance of valuing your health onto our mentee. Keep in mind that his eating and workout habits may be the result of ignorance. At risk youth are sometimes raised by people with bad habits themselves, therefore the kid literally doesn't know any other way. Encourage him to eat more nutritious foods and to eat bad food in moderation. Encourage physical activity of any kind and educate them on how to build healthy habits. This extends beyond physical health. Mental health is equally important. Teach them how to deal with stress, how to process negative thoughts and help them to develop coping skills. Mental and physical health go hand in hand. Always remember to praise him when you catch him choosing a healthy option over an unhealthy one.

You don't always get what you want: The way in which people handle disappointment can reveal a lot about their true character. Everyone is cool when life is going their way, but what happens to their attitude when things go to crap? What happens to someone when they are forced to accept life is not fair? Someday this young man is going to put his whole heart into something. It could be sports related, a part in a play, a job, a college application or a love interest. He will put all of his effort into ensuring success in this endeavor, knowing that if he just tries and works hard enough, he will come out on top. Then he will have the rug viciously pulled out from under him. He may even be forced to watch a rival be effortlessly handed the very thing he worked so hard for. Disappointing times like this call for just one thing. A "Pity Party!" Sometimes situations just suck, and it is perfectly ok to sit in it for a while. Acknowledge it, be pissed about it, then move on to the next potentially disappointing endeavor. Nobody gets their way all of the time. Sometimes you win. Sometimes you lose. How you handle victory and defeat is what is really important. Be humble in victory. Be gracious and always learn something from a defeat. Use disappointing situations to teach reflection and self evaluation. Ask him what he could have done differently. Would he have done anything differently? If the answer is no, if the kid gave it everything he had, and behaved honorably in the process, then perhaps not getting what he wanted is ok.

It's not always all about you: We all know people who are selfish, self centered, attention whores. The type of people who propose at someone else's wedding or act as though they should have been consulted before someone decided to go ahead and die on a day they had plans. People like this can be easily identified by the manner in which they hold conversations. They almost never ask questions. They suffer through other peoples annoying mouth sounds only so they can interject to spread their wisdom or tell a better story than the one they just heard. These goblins all have one thing in common. They all lack empathy, either by choice or by upbringing. If you have never been taught to consider other people and their feelings, then you won't. Encourage your mentee to ask more questions than they answer, and to really try and see things from other perspectives. Teach them that sometimes in life you are a participant and sometimes you are a spectator, because it's not always all about you.

It is ok to say "I don't know": Knowledge and wisdom are different things. Knowledge is knowing the answer to a question when asked. Wisdom is being able to admit you don't know the answer, then finding the information so the next time you are asked that same question, you can confidently and correctly answer it. Simple right? Nope! Curiously enough, lots of people confidently answer questions with absolutely no idea what the correct answer is. Can you imagine the damage these fools have caused collectively, over time? Saying "I don't know" does not mean you are stupid, it simply means you don't know the answer yet. Pretending to know something without actually learning about it is stupid. Make sure the young man you are mentoring knows the difference between knowledge and wisdom, and make sure they know that it is ok to say "I don't know".

Love is a feeling and a choice: If your mentee was raised around abusive relationships, he may not be able to recognize when he is in one or know what to do about it. He may feel like, if you love someone, you stay with them, no matter what. Worse yet, he may think that love and abuse go hand and hand. Not everyone knows or realizes that love is a feeling and a choice. He may not be able to choose who he falls in love with, but he can choose how he allows them to treat him, and if that person is bad for him, make sure he knows he can choose to leave, even if it hurts his heart.

Love is a feeling, and a young man can fall in and out of love lots of times. Give him the wisdom he needs in order to identify the one he should choose to stay in love with.

Perception is reality: One of the hardest things to get a young man to understand, is that sometimes you need to choose to cut people you care about out of your life. I am specifically referring to friends they grew up with that have chosen to become criminals, gang members, or forever children with no ambition. When explaining the need to separate themselves from people like this, you will inevitably be told "Well, I don't do any of that stuff, I just hang out with them." This is when the "Perception is Reality" talk needs to take place. The fact that he doesn't participate in criminality or hooliganism is great, but being associated with those who do, especially in the eyes of law enforcement means you are part of that group/gang. Not only that, but people in the community talk to each other and form opinions based on what friend group others keep. Encourage your mentee to attempt pulling their friend out of whatever detrimental lifestyle they have fallen into, but if their buddy does not want to change, it is ok to let him go. You can still care about someone, and recognize that they are no good for you. It is ok to look out for yourself and your own reputation.

It is ok to not be ok: Real men don't cry. We shove our feelings and emotions deep down inside. We build walls, close doors, burn bridges, and avoid painful conversations. We push our loved ones away when we feel vulnerable. We can't allow them to see our weakness. All of these tropes about how "real men" act is fragile masculinity at its finest. This, in my opinion, is weak bullshit. It takes a strong man to be vulnerable, and confide in people. It takes a real man to swallow his foolish pride, and admit he needs help dealing with something. In short, it is ok for a man to not be ok. Teach this to every young man you can. All of this fake macho garbage is bad for everyone. It causes family strife, unnecessary suffering, ulcers, and heart attacks. Stop it!

"No such thing as spare time.
No such thing as free time.
No such thing as down time.
All you get is a life time.
GO!"
-Henry Rollins

Praise & Admonishment

"Admonish your friends privately,
but praise them openly."
-Publilius Syrus

Have you ever been yelled at or ridiculed by a superior in front of other people? How did it make you feel? Did you learn anything, or did it just cause you to hate the person doing the admonishing? Nobody has a more fragile ego than a teenage boy, so doing this to them can permanently damage your relationship, if not end it. Nobody has ever learned anything by being embarrassed and screamed at. I am not a proponent of yelling at anyone, ever, but if you need to correct your mentee, pull them aside. Talk to them, and make them understand the situation, and why what they did was the wrong choice. Ask them questions about their thought process and what lead them to that conclusion. Use mistakes as teachable moments. Something else to consider is the possibility the kid is seeking negative attention on purpose. If the only attention he has ever received is negative attention, then acting up or acting out may be the only way they know how to be noticed, seen, and acknowledged by the adults in their life.

On the opposite side of the coin. When the young man does something praise worthy, even something small. Make sure everyone hears you congratulate him. Positive reenforcement works. People respond to praise. It feels good to be told you are doing great by someone you respect. This can all be boiled down to a simple phrase. Praise in public and punish in private. This is an important leadership skill to engrain into the young man you are mentoring. Coaches I respect the most are not the ones I see grabbing face masks and yelling at players on the sidelines. They are the ones who remain calm when a player makes a bonehead play, an error, or a poor decision. I respect coaches who offer words of encouragement in those moments then teach the kid in the locker room or at the next practice. We should take that same approach as Mantors.

"For me, success is not about wins and losses.
It's about helping these young fellas be the best
versions of themselves on and off the field.
And it in't always easy, but neither is growing up
without someone believing in you."
-Theodore 'Ted' Lasso

Conclusion

I am under no illusion that this book will be a life changing New York Times best seller. Hell, it's so short, I'm not even sure it qualifies as a book. I do hope this book has inspired you to get involved in the life of a young person. Every kindness you show and every lesson you teach matters. Showing a young man how to tie a tie or staging mock job interviews today, may help them land a career position tomorrow. Every kid can use another person in their corner cheering them on. Every kid needs positive adults they can look up to and emulate. Every kid needs grownups they can trust to give them sound advice. Every kid needs a Mantor.

Thank you so much for taking time out of your life to read my book.

"People will forget what you said.
People will forget what you did.
But people will never forget
how you made them feel."
-Maya Angelou